Spenser and the ROCKS

I Wonder Why

Spenser and the ROCKS

By **Lawrence F. Lowery**

Illustrated By June Goldsborough

National Science Teachers Association

National Science Teachers Association

Claire Reinburg, Director
Jennifer Horak, Managing Editor
Andrew Cooke, Senior Editor
Amanda O'Brien, Associate Editor
Wendy Rubin, Associate Editor
Amy America, Book Acquisitions Coordinator

ART AND DESIGN
Will Thomas Jr., Director
Joseph Butera, Cover, Interior Design
Original illustrations by June Goldsborough

PRINTING AND PRODUCTION
Catherine Lorrain, Director

NATIONAL SCIENCE TEACHERS ASSOCIATION
David L. Evans, Executive Director
David Beacom, Publisher

1840 Wilson Blvd., Arlington, VA 22201
www.nsta.org/store
For customer service inquiries, please call 800-277-5300.

Lexile® measure: 550L

NSTA is committed to publishing material that promotes the best in inquiry-based science education. However, conditions of actual use may vary, and the safety procedures and practices described in this book are intended to serve only as a guide. Additional precautionary measures may be required. NSTA and the authors do not warrant or represent that the procedures and practices in this book meet any safety code or standard of federal, state, or local regulations. NSTA and the authors disclaim any liability for personal injury or damage to property arising out of or relating to the use of this book, including any of the recommendations, instructions, or materials contained therein.

Library of Congress Cataloging-in-Publication Data
Lowery, Lawrence F.
  Spenser and the rocks / by Lawrence F. Lowery ; illustrated by June Goldsborough.
    pages cm -- (I wonder why)
  Summary: "Spenser and the rocks is part of the I Wonder Why book series, written to ignite the curiosity of children in grades K-6 while encouraging them to become avid readers. In addition to the information pertaining to rocks, the heart of the story is a young boy named Spenser and his interests, curiosity, and thoughts. Through the story, the reader is introduced to scientific procedures such as classification, research, and reclassification. Spenser's interest in rocks increases as he learns more about them by sorting the rocks, asking questions, and reading reference books"--Provided by publisher.
  Audience: K to grade 3.
  ISBN 978-1-938946-11-0 -- ISBN 978-1-938946-73-8 (e-book) 1. Rocks--Juvenile literature. 2. Rocks--Classification--Juvenile literature. I. Goldsborough, June, illustrator. II. National Science Teachers Association. III. Title.
  QE432.2.L684 2013
  552--dc23
                              2013020297

Cataloging-in-Publication Data are also available from the Library of Congress for the e-book.
e-LCCN: 2013025166

Introduction

The *I Wonder Why* books are science books created specifically for young learners who are in their first years of school. The content for each book was chosen to be appropriate for youngsters who are beginning to construct knowledge of the world around them. These youngsters ask questions. They want to know about things. They are more curious than they will be when they are a decade older. Research shows that science is students' favorite subject when they enter school for the first time.

Science is both *what* we know and *how* we come to know it. What we know is the content knowledge that accumulates over time as scientists continue to explore the universe in which we live. How we come to know science is the set of thinking and reasoning processes we use to get answers to the questions and inquiries in which we are engaged.

Scientists learn by observing, comparing, and organizing the objects and ideas they are investigating. Children learn the same way. These thinking processes are among several inquiry behaviors that enable us to find out about our world and how it works. Observing, comparing, and organizing are fundamental to the more advanced thinking processes of relating, experimenting, and inferring.

The five books in this set of the *I Wonder Why* series focus on Earth science content. The materials of our Earth are mostly in the forms of solids (rocks and minerals), liquids (water), and gases (air). Inquiries about these materials are initiated by curiosity. When we don't know something about an area of interest, we try to understand it by asking questions and doing investigations. These five Earth science books are written from the learner's point of view: *How Does the Wind Blow?*; *Clouds, Rain, Clouds Again*; *Spenser*

and the Rocks; *Environments of Our Earth*; and *Up, Up in a Balloon*. Children inquire about pebbles and rocks, rain and wind, and jungles and deserts. Their curiosity leads them to ask questions about land forms, weather, and climate.

The information in these books leads the characters and the reader to discover how wind can be measured and how powerful it can be, how the water cycle works, that living things need water to survive, and that plants and animals have adapted to different climate-related environments. They also learn how people have learned to fly in the ocean of air that surrounds Earth.

Each book uses a different approach to take the reader through simple scientific information. One book is expository, providing factual information. Several are narratives that allow a story to unfold. Another provides a historical perspective that tells how we gradually learn science through experimentations over time. The combination of different artwork, literary perspectives, and scientific knowledge brings the content to the reader through several instructional avenues.

In addition, the content in these books correlates to criteria set forth by national standards. Often the content is woven into each book so that its presence is subtle but powerful. The science activities in the Parent/Teacher Handbook section in each book enable learners to carry out their own investigations that relate to the content of the book. The materials needed for these activities are easily obtained, and the activities have been tested with youngsters to be sure they are age appropriate.

After students have completed a science activity, rereading or referring back to the book and talking about connections with the activity can be a deepening experience that stabilizes the learning as a long-term memory.

Spenser was a boy who, like most children, collected things. He had been collecting all kinds of things for a long time. But he was beginning to get tired of the same old things.

When the school year ended, there was not much to do.
He just kicked around trying to think of something to do.

One day, Spenser picked up a rock and wiped the dirt from it. At first the rock looked like any other rock. But the more Spenser wiped the rock, the more interesting the rock became.

Suddenly, a spot on the rock began to glitter in the Sun. Tiny flecks that looked like glass were stuck in the rock. Spenser began to wonder if all rocks had hidden surprises.

Spenser looked for rocks of different colors, shapes, and sizes. Everywhere he went, he found new and unusual rocks. He found them along the road, in fields, and on beaches.

The prettiest rocks, he thought, were beside small
streams. He would hold the rocks in the water.
When the rocks were wet, the colors looked brighter.

Spenser became more and more curious about rocks.

What were they made of?

Where did they come from?

Why were there so many different kinds?

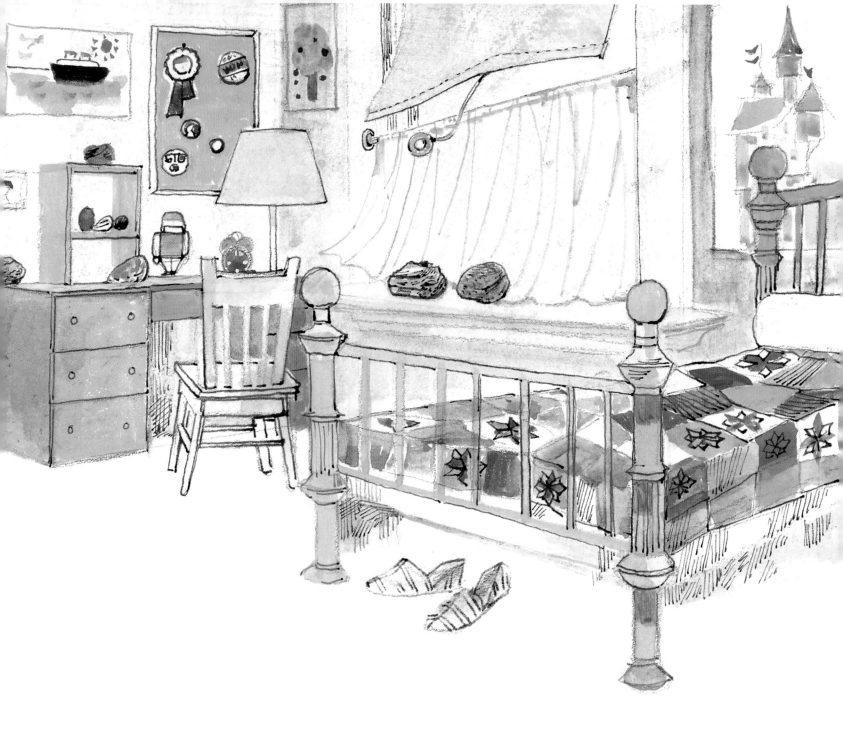

He wondered. And he kept adding rocks to his collection.

Spenser's collection became bigger and bigger. Soon he had rocks all over his room. Spenser enjoyed arranging his rocks.

He put all the red rocks together, all the black together, all the gray together, all the pink together, and all the white together.

He said to himself, "What a great collection!"

One day, Spenser wondered
what else he could do with his
collection.

He noticed the rocks were
different in other ways
besides color.

Some were rough.

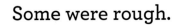

Some were smooth.

Some were soft.

Some were hard.

Some were heavy, and some were light.

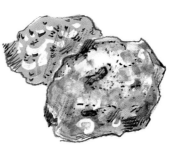

Some were dull.

Some were bright.

Spenser arranged his collection in many new ways.

One morning, he put all the rocks gathered from the same place together. Then he put rocks of the same size together. Later he put rocks he found on the same day together.

Spenser enjoyed thinking
of new ways to arrange
his rocks.

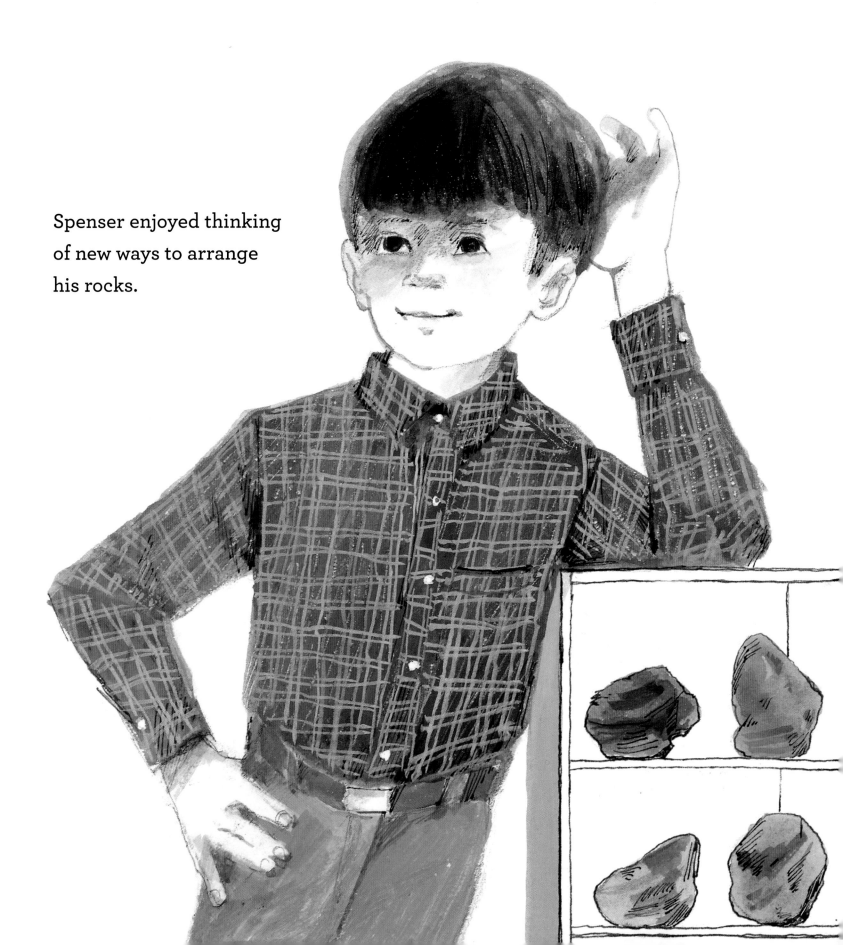

Spenser began collecting questions as well as rocks.

The questions were about rocks.

He asked his mother some questions.

He asked his father other questions.

He had questions for everyone he met.

Spenser asked so many questions that his mother
took him to the library to find some answers.

At the library, Spenser asked for a book on rocks.

He was surprised. There was not only *a* book on
rocks—there were *dozens* of books on rocks!

"Are you going to be a geologist?" the librarian asked Spenser.

Spenser said he did not know what a geologist was. The librarian told him that geologists are people who study rocks.

Spenser took home one book
and one magazine.

"I am going to be a geologist," Spenser said when he walked in the door.

He told his mother about the librarian who helped him, then showed her what he had brought home.

Spenser and his mother sat down together and studied the book. They looked at the pictures of rocks. Some of the rocks were just like the rocks Spenser had. He was interested in all of them.

Spenser's mother pointed to one picture. "This rock looks just like the one you have. It's called tuff. 'Tuff is a soft rock that comes from a volcano,'" she read. "'It is so soft, you can scratch it with your fingernail.'"

Then she pointed to another picture.

"That rock is another one that came from a volcano," she said. "It is called basalt."

Then she pointed to another one and said, "Graphite is another soft rock. It is used in pencils."

GRAPHITE

Spenser pointed to the next few pictures. His mother read on, "'Here is another soft rock—gypsum. It is used to make plaster and paint.'"

GYPSUM

CORUNDUM

"'And this rock is one of the hardest in the world. It is called corundum. Only a diamond is harder than this rock.'"

One page in the book had a chart showing pictures of rocks.

Spenser's mother read the name of each rock.

CALCITE

FLUORITE

APATITE

FELDSPAR

QUARTZ

TOPAZ

CORUNDUM

DIAMOND

Later Spenser copied down the names of rocks he had.

He learned to say the names and write them.

Soon Spenser had even more rocks in his room.
Now he was doing more than just looking at them.
He was even doing more than arranging them.
He was discovering many things about his rocks.

"Maybe, just maybe, someday I'll know more about rocks than anyone else in the whole world," Spenser thought as he watched a small ladybug crawl across his desk.

"Hey! I wonder if bugs are as interesting as rocks ..."

Spenser and the

PARENT/TEACHER HANDBOOK

Introduction

Spenser and the Rocks is about a young boy and his interests, curiosity, and thoughts. Through the story, the reader is introduced to scientific procedures such as classification, research, and reclassification. Spenser's interest in rocks increases as he learns more about them by sorting the rocks, asking questions, and reading reference books.

Inquiry Processes

This book is a narrative that focuses on character development. Spenser undergoes changes in his thinking and knowledge as he explores the properties of rocks. It is interesting how Spenser is different at the end of the story compared with the beginning. Readers might search for the factors that bring about these changes.

Organizing the objects of our world is an important aspect of science. Organizing helps scientists make sense of how things are related. As new objects are found, they are added to appropriate groupings. If there is no appropriate grouping, the arrangement is adjusted to include them. The process of organizing and reorganizing in the light of new information is a part of all sciences, and it is used to classify plants, animals, elements, or rocks.

Content

Our Earth is made up of many different materials. Rocks are the solid earth materials that compose the bulk of the landforms of our planet. There are thousands of kinds of rocks that differ in the properties geologists use to identify and distinguish them. Rocks differ in color, texture, hardness, weight, composition, and luster. According to their properties, rocks are often sorted and seriated by those properties. For example, rocks vary in hardness. Scientists have developed a scale that helps identify types of rocks based on their hardness.

Another way to group is by their method of origin. Geologists classify rocks in three divisions: igneous, sedimentary, and metamorphic.

Igneous rocks are formed from the cooling and hardening of hot molten rock from within the Earth's crust. Granite, basalt, and pumice are examples of igneous rocks.

Sedimentary rocks are formed by the cementing together of materials such as sand, mud, clay, and pebbles. As a result, this type of rock gives a banded, layered appearance. Sandstone and limestone are examples of sedimentary rocks.

Metamorphic rocks are formed by the changing of existing rocks into new kinds of rocks. This change is a result of greatly increased pressure, high temperatures, or both. Marble (which is derived from limestone) and quartzite (which is derived from sandstone) are examples of metamorphic rocks.

Science Activities

Collecting Rocks

Start a rock collection. Go outside and find a dozen different rocks. Look for rocks that have interesting properties. If possible, observe details of the rocks with a hand lens. Sort the rocks using a particular criterion (e.g., small to large, light to heavy, rough to smooth). When you finish, ask someone to look at your grouping and figure out what basis you used to group the rocks.

Decide how your rock collection might be displayed. How would you arrange the rocks in the display (e.g., by color, size, shape, or texture)? When you find more rocks to add to your collection, place them in categories you already have or reorganize the collection differently so you can include different rocks. Shoe boxes and egg cartons work well for storing and displaying rocks and can be labeled accordingly (e.g., smooth rocks, red rocks, sedimentary rocks). Individual labels (e.g., shale, quartz) can be added after checking reference books or identification keys.

Examining Some Properties of Rocks

Rub one rock against another. What happens? Do this with different rocks. Use a hand lens to examine the particles that are rubbed away. When you rub two different rocks together, is one rock harder than the other? Can you arrange the rocks in your collection on the basis of hardness? Find out why some rocks are smooth and some are rough.

Seriating Rocks by Size

Scientists have learned a lot about rocks by seriating the rocks, making a table of how they were seriated, and labeling each part of the seriation. For example, when rocks are seriated by their sizes, scientists use a size scale. In 1922, Chester K. Wentworth modified an earlier scale by Johan A. Udden. Wentworth's types of rocks and sizes have been improved several times since then. Here is a simplified version of the Wentworth Scale.

Type of Rock	Size in Millimeters (mm)
boulder	larger than 256 mm
cobble	64–256 mm
pebble	4–64 mm
gravel	2–4 mm
very coarse sand	1–2 mm
coarse sand	0.5–1 mm
medium sand	0.25–0.5 mm
fine sand	0.125–0.25 mm
very fine sand	0.062–0.125 mm
silt	0.004–0.062 mm
clay	smaller than 0.004 mm

Rocks larger than sand (gravel, pebbles, cobbles, and boulders) are collectively called gravel, and rocks smaller than fine sand (silt and clay) are collectively called mud.

Find an example of each size of rock near where you live.